LIVING THE YEAR OF THE EUCHARIST

LIVING THE YEAR OF THE EUCHARIST

JOSEMARÍA ESCRIVÁ

WITH A PREFACE BY
JAVIER ECHEVARRÍA

Copyright © 2005 Scepter Publishers, Inc.
All rights reserved

Scepter Publishers, Inc.
P.O. Box 211, New York, NY 10018
www.scepterpublishers.org

ISBN 1–59417–036–3

Text composed in Century and Copperplate fonts

First Printing
Printed in the United States of America

Preface

by Javier Echevarría

7

THE EUCHARIST:
MYSTERY OF FAITH AND LOVE

by St. Josemaría Escrivá

13

ON THE FEAST
OF
CORPUS CHRISTI

by St. Josemaría Escrivá

33

Notes

51

Preface

This booklet contains two homilies of St. Josemaría Escrivá on the Holy Eucharist. The first considers this mystery as a sacrifice and as communion—the Holy Mass. The second looks at it as a sacrament worthy of adoration—the Real Presence outside of Mass. Both were published in one of the collections of homilies by Opus Dei's founder (*Christ Is Passing By*). Their publication here in a booklet, however, can help the faithful to draw greater profit from the Eucharistic Year proclaimed by the Holy Father John Paul II, lasting from October 2004 to October 2005.

In his Apostolic letter *Mane Nobiscum Domine*, dated October 7, 2004, the Pope says: "If the only result of this Year were the revival in all Christian communities of the celebration of Sunday Mass and an increase in Eucharistic worship outside Mass, this Year of grace would be abundantly successful" (no. 29).

These pages transmit the experience of a saint deeply in love with Jesus Christ, and therefore ardently devoted to the Blessed Sacrament. I had the good fortune, a real grace from God, to live at his side for many years. Thus I had frequent opportunity to contemplate from close-up his strong, tender and contagious faith, grounded on Catholic doctrine, and enkindled by love for God, even when, as happens to all of us, that love was not accompanied by sensible feelings.

Anyone who had the opportunity to see St. Josemaría celebrate Holy Mass, or to witness how he genuflected before the tabernacle, or simply how he looked lovingly at the Sacred Host exposed in the monstrance, was deeply moved. So great was his faith in the real presence of Jesus Christ in the Eucharist that he was often led to exclaim: "Lord, I believe in you, in the marvel of love that is your Real Presence beneath the Eucharistic species after the consecration, on the altar and in the tabernacles where you are reserved. I believe more firmly than if I heard you with my ears, than if I saw you with my eyes, than if I touched you with my hands" (*Letter*, March 28, 1973, no. 7).

That huge, unshakable faith was a divine gift, to which the founder of Opus Dei always corresponded, with complete trust in God. Often, when he spoke about the mystery of the Eucharist, he used examples taken from human love, since (as he himself lived and tirelessly preached) we only have one heart with which to love God—the same heart with which we love those closest to us.

If we deal with Jesus Christ in this way, we will discover that the Blessed Sacrament "summarizes all that Christ asks of us" (*Christ Is Passing By*, no. 88). We will learn how to deal with each of the divine Persons. We will learn how to serve the others, forgetting about ourselves. And we will learn how to divinize our entire day, converting it, as St. Josemaría taught, into "a Mass" that is both a prolongation of and a preparation for the Holy Sacrifice, which we Catholics have to be present at and participate in actively.

The Eucharist is a *mystery of light,* as the Pope emphasized when including it in the Holy Rosary. This light of Christ has to illuminate every moment of our life: our intense work, at times going against the grain; our family life, with its joys and sorrows; social relations; moments dedicated to resting; periods of sickness. Everything is an occasion for encountering God if our life is "essentially, totally Eucharistic" (*The Forge*, no. 826).

I ask our Lady that reading and meditating on these writings of the founder of Opus Dei may illumine the conduct of many men and women. May his words enkindle their hearts with love for God and spur them—as it did the disciples on their way to Emmaus (Lk 24)—to communicate to others the good news of their meeting with Christ who has died and risen, and who is now glorious, truly present in the Most Holy Sacrament of the Altar.

The Virgin Mary welcomed the Word made flesh into her virginal womb; she carried him beneath her heart for nine months, cradled him in her arms, and contemplated him with love. Our Lady, the Mediatrix of all graces, will obtain for us from the Blessed Trinity the gift that we all hope for in this Year of the Eucharist: a closer intimacy with her Son, Jesus, who renews his redeeming sacrifice on the altar sacramentally, and awaits us in the tabernacle.

+ Javier Echevarría
Prelate of Opus Dei

HOMILIES

THE EUCHARIST: MYSTERY OF FAITH AND LOVE

A homily given on April 14, 1960

"Now before the feast of the Passover, when Jesus knew that his hour had come to depart out of this world to the Father, having loved his own who were in the world, he loved them to the end."[1] The reader of this verse from Saint John's Gospel is brought to understand that a great event is about to take place. The introduction, full of tender affection, is similar to that which we find in Saint Luke: "I have earnestly desired," says our Lord, "to eat this Passover with you before I suffer."[2]

Let us begin by asking the Holy Spirit, from this moment on, to give us the grace to understand every word and gesture of Christ. Because we want to live a supernatural life, because our Lord has shown his desire to give himself to us as nourishment for our soul, and because we acknowledge that only he has "words of eternal life."[3]

Faith makes us profess in the words of Peter that "we have come to believe and to know that you are the Christ, the Son of God."[4] It is this faith, together with our devotion, that leads us to emulate the daring of John, to come close to Jesus and to rest on the breast of the Master,[5] who loved those who were with him ardently, and who was to love them, as we have just read, to the end.

Any words we might use to explain the mystery of Holy Thursday are inadequate. But it is not hard to imagine the feelings of Jesus' heart on that evening, his last evening with his friends before the sacrifice of Calvary.

Think of the human experience of two people who love each other, and yet are forced to part. They would like to stay together forever, but duty—in one form or another—forces them to separate. They are unable to fulfill their desire of remaining close to each other, so man's love—which, great as it may be, is limited—seeks a symbolic gesture. People who make their farewells exchange gifts or perhaps a photograph with a dedication so ardent that it seems almost enough to burn that piece of paper. They can do no more, because a creature's power is not so great as its desire.

What we cannot do, our Lord is able to do. Jesus Christ, perfect God and perfect man, leaves us, not a symbol, but a reality. He himself stays with us. He will go to the Father, but he will also remain among men. He will leave us, not simply a gift that will make us remember him, not an image that becomes blurred with time, like a photograph that soon fades and yellows, and has no meaning except for those who were contemporaries. Under the appearances of bread and wine, he is really present, with his body and blood, with his soul and divinity.

THE JOY OF HOLY THURSDAY

How well we understand the song that Christians of all times have unceasingly sung to the Sacred Host: "Sing, my tongue, the mystery of the glorious body and of the precious blood, that the king of all nations, born of the generous womb of the Virgin, has offered for the redemption of the world."[6] We must adore devoutly this God of ours, hidden in the Eucharist[7]—it is Jesus himself, born of the Virgin Mary, who suffered and gave his life in the sacrifice of the cross; Jesus, from whose side, pierced by a lance, flowed water and blood.[8]

This is the sacred banquet, in which we receive Christ himself. We renew the memory of his Passion, and through him the soul is brought to an intimate relationship with God and receives a promise of future glory.[9] The liturgy of the Church has summarized, in a few words, the culminating points of the history of our Lord's love for us.

The God of our faith is not a distant being who contemplates indifferently the fate of men—their desires, their struggles, their sufferings. He is a Father who loves his children so much that he sends the Word, the Second Person of the most Blessed Trinity, so that by taking on the nature of man he may die to redeem us. He is the loving

Father who now leads us gently to himself, through the action of the Holy Spirit who dwells in our hearts.

This is the source of the joy we feel on Holy Thursday—the realization that the creator has loved his creatures to such an extent. Our Lord Jesus Christ, as though all the other proofs of his mercy were insufficient, institutes the Eucharist so that he can always be close to us. We can only understand up to a point that he does so because Love moves him, who needs nothing, not to want to be separated from us. The Blessed Trinity has fallen in love with man, raised to the level of grace and made "to God's image and likeness." [10] God has redeemed him from sin—from the sin of Adam, inherited by all his descendants, as well as from his personal sins—and desires ardently to dwell in his soul: "If anyone love me, he will keep my word; and my Father will love him, and we will come to him and make our abode with him." [11]

THE EUCHARIST AND
THE MYSTERY OF THE TRINITY

The Blessed Trinity's love for man is made permanent in a sublime way through the Eucharist. Many years ago, we all learned from our catechism that the Eucharist can be considered as a sacrifice and as a sacrament; and that the sacrament is present to us both in Communion and as a treasure on the altar, in the tabernacle. The Church dedicates another feast to the eucharistic mystery—the feast of the body of Christ, Corpus Christi, present in all the tabernacles of the world. Today, on Holy Thursday, we can turn our attention to the holy Eucharist as our sacrifice and as our nourishment, in the holy Mass and in Communion.

I was talking to you about the love of the Blessed Trinity for man. And where can we see this more clearly than in the Mass? The three divine Persons act together in the holy sacrifice of the altar. This is why I like to repeat the final words of the collect, secret, and postcommunion: "Through Jesus Christ, your Son, our Lord," we pray to God the Father, "who lives and reigns with you in the unity of the Holy Spirit, one God, forever and ever. Amen."

In the Mass, our prayer to God the Father is constant. The priest represents the eternal high priest, Jesus Christ, who is, at the same time, the victim offered in this sacrifice. And the action of the Holy Spirit in the Mass is truly present, although in a mysterious manner. "By the power of the Holy Spirit," writes Saint John Damascene, "the transformation of the bread into the body of Christ takes place." [12]

The action of the Holy Spirit is clearly expressed when the priest invokes the divine blessing on the offerings: "Come, Sanctifier, almighty and eternal God, and bless this sacrifice prepared in honor of your holy name" [13]—the holocaust that will give to the holy name of God the glory that is due. The sanctification we pray for is attributed to the Paraclete, who is sent to us by the Father and the Son. And we also recognize the active presence of the Holy Spirit in this sacrifice, as we say, shortly before Communion: "Lord Jesus Christ, who, by the will of the Father, with the cooperation of the Holy Spirit, by your death have brought life to the world. . . ."[14]

The three divine Persons are present in the sacrifice of the altar. By the will of the Father, with the cooperation of the Holy Spirit, the Son offers himself in a redemptive sacrifice. We learn how to personalize our relationship with the most Blessed Trinity, one God in three Persons: three divine Persons in the unity of God's substance, in the unity of his love and of his sanctifying action.

Immediately after the Lavabo, the priest prays: "Receive, Holy Trinity, this offering that we make in memory of the Passion, Resurrection and Ascension of our Lord Jesus Christ."[15] And, at the end of the Mass, there is another prayer of homage to the Trinity of God: "May the tribute of my service be pleasing to you, O Holy Trinity; and grant the sacrifice that I, who am unworthy, have offered to your majesty, may be acceptable to you; and that through your mercy it may bring forgiveness to me and to all those for whom I have offered it."[16]

The Mass is, I insist, an action of God, of the Trinity. It is not a merely human event. The priest who celebrates fulfills the desire of our Lord, lending his body and his voice to the divine action. He acts, not in his own name, but *in persona et in nomine Christi*: in the Person of Christ and in his name.

Because of the Blessed Trinity's love for man, the presence of Christ in the Eucharist brings all graces to the Church and to mankind. This is the sacrifice announced by the prophet Malachy: "From the rising of the sun to its setting my name is great among the nations, and a fragrant sacrifice and a pure offering is made to me in all places."[17] It is the sacrifice of Christ, offered to the Father with the cooperation of the Holy Spirit—an offering of infinite value, which perpetuates the work of the redemption in us and surpasses the sacrifices of the old law.

HOLY MASS IN THE CHRISTIAN'S LIFE

The holy Mass brings us face to face with one of the central mysteries of our faith, because it is the gift of the Blessed Trinity to the Church. It is because of this that we can consider the Mass as the center and the source of a Christian's spiritual life.

It is the aim of all the sacraments.[18] The life of grace, into which we are brought by Baptism, and which is increased and strengthened by Confirmation, grows to its fullness in the Mass. "When we participate in the Eucharist," writes Saint Cyril of Jerusalem, "we are made spiritual by the divinizing action of the Holy Spirit, who not only makes us share in Christ's life, as in Baptism, but makes us entirely Christ-like, incorporating us into the fullness of Christ Jesus." [19]

This pouring out of the Holy Spirit unites us to Christ and makes us acknowledge that we are children of God. The Paraclete, who is Love, teaches us to saturate our life with the virtue of charity. Thus *consummati in unum*: "made one with Christ," [20] we can be among men what the Eucharist is for us, in the words of Saint Augustine: "a sign of unity, a bond of love." [21]

I will not surprise anyone if I say that some Christians have a very poor concept of the holy Mass. For them it is a purely external rite, if not a mere social convention. This is because our poor hearts are capable of treating the greatest gift of God to man as routine. In the Mass, in this Mass that we are now celebrating, the most Holy Trinity intervenes, I repeat, in a very special way. To correspond to such great love, we must give ourselves completely, in body and in soul. We hear God, we talk to him, we see him, we taste him. And when words are not enough, we sing, urging our tongue—*Pange, lingua!*—to proclaim to all mankind the greatness of the Lord.

To *live* the holy Mass means to pray continually, and to be convinced that, for each one of us, this is a personal meeting with God. We adore him, we praise him, we give thanks to him, we atone for our sins, we are purified, we feel ourselves united in Christ with all Christians.

We may have asked ourselves, at one time or another, how we can correspond to the greatness of God's love. We may have wanted to see a program for Christian living clearly explained. The answer is easy, and it is within reach of all the faithful: to participate lovingly in the holy Mass, to learn to deepen our personal relationship with God in the sacrifice that summarizes all that Christ asks of us.

Let me remind you of what you have seen on so many occasions: the succession of prayers and actions as they unfold before our eyes at Mass. As we follow them, step by step, our Lord may show us aspects of our lives in which each one of us must improve, vices we must conquer, and the kind of brotherly attitude that we should develop with regard to all men.

The priest draws near to the altar of God, "of God who gives joy to our youth." The holy Mass begins with a song of joy, because God is here. It is the joy that is shown, together with love and gratitude, as the priest kisses the altar, symbol of Christ and reminder of the saints—a small surface, sanctified because this is where the sacrament of infinite worth is made present to us.

The Confiteor makes us aware of our unworthiness; not an abstract reminder of guilt, but the actual presence of our sins and weaknesses. This is why we repeat: *Kyrie, eleison, Christe, eleison:* Lord, have mercy, Christ, have mercy. If the forgiveness we need had to be won by our own merits, we would only be capable of a bitter sadness. But, because of God's goodness, forgiveness comes from his mercy, and we praise him—*Gloria!*: "for you alone are the holy one, you alone are Lord, you alone, O Jesus Christ, are the most high, with the Holy Spirit in the glory of God the Father."

We now listen to the word of Scripture, the Epistle and the Gospel—light from the Holy Spirit, who speaks through human voices so as to make our intellect come to know and contemplate, to strengthen our will and make our desire for action effective. And because we are one people, "gathered together in the unity of the Father, and of the Son, and of the Holy Spirit,"[22] we recite the Creed, affirming the unity of our faith.

Then, the offering: the bread and wine of men. It is very little, but it is accompanied by prayer: "Lord God, we ask you to receive us and be pleased with the sacrifice we offer you with humble and contrite hearts: and that the sacrifice which today we offer you, O God, our Lord, may be brought to your presence and be made acceptable." Again, a reminder of our smallness and of the desire to cleanse and purify all that is offered to God: "I will wash my hands . . . I have loved the beauty of your house."

A moment ago, just before the Lavabo, we invoked the Holy Spirit, asking him to bless the sacrifice offered to his holy name. After washing his hands, the priest, in the name of all those present, prays to the Holy Trinity—*Suscipe, Sancta Trinitas*—to accept our offering in memory of the life of Christ and of his Passion, Resurrection and Ascension; and in honor of Mary, ever Virgin, and of all the saints.

May this offering be effective for the salvation of all men—*Orate, fratres*, the priest invites the people to pray—because this sacrifice is yours and mine, it is the sacrifice of the whole Church. Pray, brethren, although there may not be many present, although materially there may be only one person there, although the celebrant may find himself alone; because every Mass is a universal sacrifice, the redemption of every tribe and tongue and people and nation.[23]

Through the communion of the saints, all Christians receive grace from every Mass that is celebrated, regardless of whether there is an attendance of thousands of persons, or whether it is only a boy with his mind on other things who is there to serve. In either case, Heaven and earth join with the angels of the Lord to sing: *Sanctus, Sanctus, Sanctus* . . .

I adore and praise with the angels—it is not difficult, because I know that, as I celebrate the holy Mass, they surround me, adoring the Blessed Trinity. And I know that in some way the Blessed Virgin is there, because of her intimate relationship with the most Blessed Trinity and because she is the Mother of Christ, of his flesh and blood—the Mother of Jesus Christ, perfect God and perfect man. Jesus was conceived in the womb of Mary most holy, not through the intervention of man, but by the power of the Holy Spirit alone. In his veins runs the blood of his Mother, the blood that is offered in the sacrifice of the redemption, on Calvary and in the Mass.

Thus we begin the canon, with the confidence of children of God, calling him our most loving Father: *clementissime.* We pray for the Church and for all those who are a part of the Church—the pope, our families, our friends and companions. And a Catholic, with his heart open to all men, will pray for all men, because no one can be excluded from his love. We ask God to hear our prayers. We call on the memory of the glorious ever-Virgin Mary and of a handful of men who were among the first to follow Christ and to die for him, and we recall our union with them.

Quam oblationem . . . the moment of the Consecration draws near. Now, in the Mass, it is Christ who acts again, through the priest: "This is my body" . . . "This is the cup of my blood." Jesus is with us! The transubstantiation is a renewal of the miracle of God's infinite love. When that moment takes place again today, let us tell our Lord, without any need for words, that nothing will be able to separate us from him; that, as he puts himself into our hands, defenseless, under the fragile appearances of bread and wine, he has made us his willing slaves. "Make me live always through you, and taste the sweetness of your love." [24]

More prayers, because we human beings almost always feel the need to ask for things—prayers for our deceased brothers, for ourselves. We have brought all our weaknesses, our lack of faithfulness. The weight is heavy, but he wants to bear it for us and with us. The canon ends with another invocation to the Blessed Trinity: *Per ipsum, et cum ipso, et in ipso* . . . —through Christ, and with Christ, and in Christ, who is all our love, in the unity of the Holy Spirit, all honor and glory is yours, almighty Father, for ever and ever.

Jesus is the way, the mediator. In him are all things; outside of him is nothing. In Christ, taught by him, we dare to call God our Father—he is the Almighty who created Heaven and earth, and he is a loving Father who waits for us to come back to him again and again, as the story of the prodigal son repeats itself in our lives.

Ecce Agnus Dei . . . Domine, non sum dignus . . . We are going to receive our Lord. On this earth, when we receive an important person, we bring out the best—lights, music, formal dress. How should we prepare to receive Christ into our soul? Have we ever thought about how we would behave if we could only receive him once in a lifetime?

When I was a child, frequent Communion was still not a widespread practice. I remember how people used to prepare to go to Communion. Everything had to be just right, body and soul: the best clothes, hair well-combed—even physical cleanliness was important—maybe even a few drops of cologne.... These were manifestations of love, full of finesse and refinement, on the part of manly souls who knew how to repay Love with love.

With Christ in our soul, we end the holy Mass. The blessing of the Father, of the Son, and of the Holy Spirit accompanies us all day long, as we go about our simple, normal task of making holy all honest human activity.

As you attend Mass, you will learn to deepen your friendship with each one of the three divine Persons: the Father who begets the Son; the Son, begotten by the Father; the Holy Spirit, who proceeds from the Father and the Son. When we approach any one of the divine Persons, we approach the one God. And when we come close to all three Persons—Father, Son, and Holy Spirit—again we come into the presence of the one true God. Love the Mass, my children, love the Mass. And be hungry to receive our Lord in Communion, although you may be cold inside, although your emotions may not correspond to your desires. Receive Communion with faith, with hope, with burning charity.

CONTACT WITH JESUS

A man who fails to love the Mass fails to love Christ. We must make an effort to *live* the Mass with calm and serenity, with devotion and affection. Those who love acquire a finesse, a sensitivity of soul that makes them notice details that are sometimes very small, but that are important because they express the love of a passionate heart. This is how we should attend the holy Mass. And this is why I have always suspected that those who want the Mass to be over quickly show, with this insensitive attitude, that they have not yet realized what the sacrifice of the altar means.

If we love Christ, who offers himself for us, we will feel compelled to find a few minutes after Mass for an intimate personal thanksgiving, which will prolong in the silence of our hearts that other thanksgiving which is the Eucharist. How are we to approach him, what are we to say, how should we behave?

Christian life is not made up of rigid norms, because the Holy Spirit does not guide souls collectively, but inspires each one with resolutions, inspirations, and affections that will help it to recognize and fulfill the will of the Father. Still, I feel that, on many occasions, the central theme of our conversation with Christ, in our thanksgiving after holy Mass, can be the consideration that our Lord is our king, physician, teacher, and friend.

He is our king. He desires ardently to rule our hearts, because we are children of God. But we should not try to imagine a human sort of rule—Christ does not dominate or seek to impose himself, because he "has not come to be served but to serve." [25]

His kingdom is one of peace, of joy, of justice. Christ our king does not expect us to spend our time in abstract reasoning; he expects deeds, because "not everyone who says to me, 'Lord, Lord!', shall enter the kingdom of Heaven; but he who does the will of my Father in Heaven shall enter the kingdom of Heaven." [26]

He is our physician, and he heals our selfishness, if we let his grace penetrate to the depths of our soul. Jesus has taught us that the worst sickness is hypocrisy, the pride that leads us to hide our own sins. We have to be totally sincere with him. We have to tell the whole truth, and then we have to say: "Lord, if you will"—and you are always willing—"you can make me clean." [27] You know my weaknesses; I feel these symptoms; I suffer from these failings. We show him the wound, with simplicity, and if the wound is festering, we show the pus too. Lord, you have cured so many souls; help me to recognize you as the divine physician, when I have you in my heart or when I contemplate your presence in the tabernacle.

He is a teacher, with a knowledge that only he possesses—the knowledge of unlimited love for

God, and, in God, for all men. In Christ's teaching we learn that our existence does not belong to us. He gave up his life for all men and, if we follow him, we must understand that we cannot take possession of our own lives in a selfish way, without sharing the sorrows of others. Our life belongs to God. We are here to spend it in his service, concerning ourselves generously with souls, showing, through our words and our example, the extent of the Christian dedication that is expected of us.

Jesus expects us to nourish the desire to acquire this knowledge, so that he can repeat to us: "If anyone thirst, let him come to me and drink."[28] And we answer: teach us to forget ourselves, so that we may concern ourselves with you and with all souls. In this way, our Lord will lead us forward with his grace, just as when we were learning to write. Do you remember that childish scrawl, guided by the teacher's hand? And we will begin to taste the joy of showing our faith, which is yet another gift from God, and showing it with clear strokes of Christian conduct, in which all will be able to read the wonders of God.

He is our friend, *the* Friend: *vos autem dixi amicos*,[29] he says. He calls us his friends; and he is the one who took the first step, because he loved us first. Still, he does not impose his love—he offers it. He shows it with the clearest possible sign: "Greater love than this no one has, that one lay down his life for his friends."[30] He was Lazarus' friend. He wept for him when he saw him dead, and he raised him from the dead. If he sees us cold, unwilling, rigid perhaps with the stiffness of a dying interior life, his tears will be our life—"I say to you, my friend, arise and walk," [31] leave that narrow life which is no life at all.

Our Holy Thursday meditation draws to a close. If our Lord has helped us—and he is always ready to do so, as long as we open our hearts to him—we will feel the need to correspond in what is most important, and that is love. And we will know how to spread that love among other men, with a life of service. "I have given you an example," [32] he tells his disciples after washing their feet, on the night of the Last Supper. Let us reject from our hearts any pride, any ambition, any desire to dominate; and peace and joy will reign around us and within us, as a consequence of our personal sacrifice.

Finally, a loving thought directed to Mary, Mother of God and our Mother. Forgive me if I go back to another childhood memory—a picture that became very common in my own country when Saint Pius X was encouraging the practice of frequent Communion. It represented Mary adoring the sacred Host. Today, as in those days and as always, our Lady teaches us to come to Jesus, to recognize him and to find him in all the different situations of our day. And nowhere is she more a teacher than in the supreme moment of the holy sacrifice of the Mass, where time blends with eternity. Jesus, with the gesture of a high priest, attracts all things to himself and places them, with the breath of the Holy Spirit, in the presence of God the Father.

ON THE FEAST OF CORPUS CHRISTI

A homily given on May 28, 1964

Today, on the feast of Corpus Christi, we come together to consider the depths of our Lord's love for us, which has led him to stay with us, hidden under the appearances of the Blessed Sacrament. It almost seems as if we can physically hear him teaching the multitude: "A sower went out to sow his seed. And as he sowed, some seeds fell along the path, and the birds came and devoured them. Other seeds fell on rocky ground, where they had not much soil, and immediately they sprang up, since they had no depth of soil, but when the sun rose they were scorched; and since they had no root they withered away. Other seeds fell among thorns, and the thorns grew up and choked them. Other seeds fell on good soil and brought forth grain, some a hundredfold, some sixty, some thirty."[1]

It is a vivid scene. The divine sower is also sowing his seed today. The work of salvation is still going on, and our Lord wants us to share that work. He wants Christians to open to his love all the paths of the earth. He invites us to spread the divine message, by both teaching and example, to the farthest corners of the earth. He asks us, as citizens of both ecclesial and civil society, to be other Christs by fulfilling our duties conscientiously, sanctifying our everyday work and the responsibilities of our particular walk of life.

If we look around, if we take a look at the world, which we love because it is God's handiwork, we will find that the parable holds true. The word of Jesus Christ is fruitful, it stirs many souls to dedication and fidelity. The life and conduct of those who serve God have changed history. Even many of those who do not know our Lord are motivated, perhaps unconsciously, by ideals which derive from Christianity.

We can also see that some of the seed falls on barren ground or among thorns and thistles; some hearts close themselves to the light of faith. Ideals of peace, reconciliation, and brotherhood are widely accepted and proclaimed, but all too often the facts belie them. Some people are futilely bent on smothering God's voice. To drown it out they use brute force or a method which is more subtle but perhaps more cruel because it drugs the spirit, indifference.

THE BREAD OF ETERNAL LIFE

When thinking about all this, I should like us to take stock of our mission as Christians. Let's turn our eyes to the holy Eucharist, toward Jesus. He is here with us, he has made us a part of himself: "Now you are the body of Christ and individually members of it."[2] God has decided to stay in the tabernacle to nourish us, strengthen us, make us divine, and give effectiveness to our work and efforts. Jesus is at one and the same time the sower, the seed, and the final result of the sowing: the bread of eternal life.

The miracle of the holy Eucharist is being continually renewed and it has all Jesus' personal traits. Perfect God and perfect man, Lord of Heaven and earth, he offers himself to us as nourishment in the most natural and ordinary way. Love has been awaiting us for almost two thousand years. That's a long time and yet it's not, for when you are in love time flies.

I remember a lovely poem, one of the songs collected by Alfonso X the Wise. It's a legend about a simple monk who begged our Lady to let him see Heaven, even if only for a moment. Our Lady granted him his wish, and the good monk found himself in paradise. When he returned, he could not recognize the monastery—his prayer, which he had thought very short, lasted three centuries. Three centuries are nothing to a person in love. That's how I explain Christ waiting in the Eucharist. It is God waiting for us, God who loves man, who searches us out, who loves us just as we are—limited, selfish, inconstant, but capable of discovering his infinite affection and of giving ourselves fully to him.

Motivated by his own love and by his desire to teach us to love, Jesus came on earth and has stayed with us in the Eucharist. "Having loved his own who were in the world, he loved them to the end"[3]—that's how Saint John begins his account of what happened on the eve of the pasch when Jesus "took bread and after he had given thanks, broke it, and said, 'This is my body which is given up for you. Do this in remembrance of me.' In the same way also the cup, after supper, saying: 'This is the new covenant in my blood. Do this, as often as you drink it, in remembrance of me.' "[4]

A NEW LIFE

It is the simple and solemn moment of the establishment of the new alliance. Jesus dissolves the old economy of the law and reveals to us that he himself will be the content of our prayer and life. Just look at the joy which invades today's liturgy: "Let the anthem be clear and strong and full of joy."[5] It is a great Christian celebration which sings about a new era: "The old pasch is by the new replaced; the substance hath the shadow chased and rising day dispels the night."[6]

This is a miracle of love. "This is truly the bread for God's children."[7] Jesus, the first son of the eternal Father, offers us himself as food. And the same Jesus is waiting to receive us in Heaven as "his guests, his co-heirs and his fellows,"[8] for "those who are nourished by Christ will die the earthly death of time, but they will live eternally because Christ is life everlasting."[9]

Eternal happiness begins now for the Christian who is comforted with the definitive manna of the Eucharist. The old life has gone forever. Let us leave everything behind us so that everything will be new, "our hearts, our words, and our actions." [10]

This is the Good News. *News*, because it speaks to us of a deep love which we never could have dreamed of. *Good*, because there is nothing better than uniting ourselves to God, the greatest Good of all. It is *Good News*, because in an inexplicable way it gives us a foretaste of Heaven.

Jesus hides in the Blessed Sacrament of the altar because he wants us to *dare* to approach him. He wants to nourish us so we become one single thing with him. When he said, "Apart from me you can do nothing," [11] he was not condemning Christians to ineffectiveness or obliging them to seek him by a difficult and arduous route. On the contrary. He has stayed here with us, he is totally available to us.

When we gather before the altar where the holy sacrifice of the Mass is being celebrated, when we contemplate the sacred Host in the monstrance or adore it hidden in the tabernacle, our faith should be strengthened; we should reflect on this new life which we are receiving and be moved by God's affection and tenderness.

"They devoted themselves to the Apostles' teaching and fellowship, to the breaking of the bread and the prayers." [12] That is how the Scriptures describe the life of the early Christians. They were brought together by the faith of the Apostles in perfect unity, to share in the Eucharist and to pray with one mind. Faith, bread, word.

In the Eucharist Jesus gives us a sure pledge of his presence in our souls; of his power, which supports the whole world; of his promises of salvation, which will help the human family to dwell forever in the house in Heaven when time comes to an end. There we shall find God the Father, God the Son, God the Holy Spirit: the Blessed Trinity, the one and only God. Our whole faith is brought into play when we believe in Jesus, really present under the appearances of bread and wine.

I cannot see how anyone could live as a Christian and not feel the need for the constant friendship of Jesus in the word and in the bread, in prayer and in the Eucharist. And I easily understand the ways in which successive generations of faithful have expressed their love for the Eucharist, both with public devotions making profession of the faith and with silent, simple practices in the peace of a church or the intimacy of their hearts.

The important thing is that we should love the Mass and make it the center of our day. If we attend Mass well, surely we are likely to think about our Lord during the rest of the day, wanting to be always in his presence, ready to work as he worked and love as he loved. And so we learn to thank our Lord for his kindness in not limiting his presence to the time of the sacrifice of the altar. He has decided to stay with us in the Host which is reserved in the tabernacle.

For me the tabernacle has always been a Bethany, a quiet and pleasant place where Christ resides. A place where we can tell him about our worries, our sufferings, our desires, our joys, with the same sort of simplicity and naturalness as Martha, Mary, and Lazarus. That is why I rejoice when I stumble upon a church in town or in the country; it's another tabernacle, another opportunity for the soul to escape and join in intention our Lord in the Sacrament.

THE RICHNESS OF THE EUCHARIST

When our Lord instituted the Eucharist during the Last Supper, night had already fallen. This indicated, according to Saint John Chrysostom, that "the times had run their course."[13] The world had fallen into darkness, for the old rites, the old signs of God's infinite mercy to mankind, were going to be brought to fulfillment. The way was opening to a new dawn—the new pasch. The Eucharist was instituted during that night, preparing in advance for the morning of the Resurrection.

We too have to prepare for this new dawn. Everything harmful, worn out, or useless has to be thrown away—discouragement, suspicion, sadness, cowardice. The holy Eucharist gives the sons of God a divine newness and we must respond "in the newness of your mind,"[14] renewing all our feelings and actions. We have been given a new principle of energy, strong new roots grafted onto our Lord. We must not return to the old leaven, for now we have the bread which lasts forever.

On this feast of Corpus Christi, in cities and towns throughout the world, Christians accompany our Lord in procession. Hidden in the Host he moves through the streets and squares—just as during his earthly life—going to meet those who want to see him, making himself available to those who are not looking for him. And so, once more, he comes among his own people. How are we to respond to this call of his?

The external signs of love should come from the heart and find expression in the testimony of a Christian life. If we have been renewed by receiving our Lord's body, we should *show* it. Let us pray that our thoughts be sincere, full of peace, self-giving, and service. Let us pray that we be true and clear in what we say—the right thing at the right time—so as to console and help and especially bring God's light to others. Let us pray that our actions be consistent and effective and right, so that they give off "the good fragrance of Christ,"[15] evoking his way of doing things.

The Corpus Christi procession makes Christ present in towns and cities throughout the world. But his presence cannot be limited to just one day, a noise you hear and then forget. It should remind us that we have to discover our Lord in our ordinary everyday activity. Side by side with this solemn procession, there is the simple, silent procession of the ordinary life of each Christian. He is a man among men, who by good fortune has received the faith and the divine commission to act so that he renews the message of our Lord on earth. We are not without defects; we make mistakes and commit sins. But God is with us and we must make ourselves ready to be used by him, so that he can continue to walk among men.

Let us ask our Lord, then, to make us souls devoted to the blessed Eucharist, so that our relationship with him brings forth joy and serenity and a desire for justice. In this way we will make it easier for others to recognize Christ; we will put Christ at the center of all human activities. And Jesus' promise will be fulfilled: "I, when I am lifted up from the earth, will draw all men to myself." [16]

Jesus, as we were saying, is the sower, and he goes about his task by means of us Christians. Christ presses the grain in his wounded hands, soaks it in his blood, cleans it, purifies it, and throws it into the furrows, into the world. He plants the seeds one by one so that each Christian in his own setting can bear witness to the fruitfulness of the death and Resurrection of the Lord.

If we are in Christ's hands, we should absorb his saving blood and let ourselves be cast on the wind. We should accept our life as God wants it.

And we should be convinced that the seed must be buried and die[17] if it is to be fruitful. Then the shoots start to appear, and the grain. And from the grain, bread is made which is changed by God into the body of Christ. In this way we once more become united with Jesus, our sower. "Because there is one bread, we who are many are one body, for we all partake of the one bread."[18]

We should always remember that if there is no sowing there is no harvest. That is why we need to sow the word of God generously, to make Christ known to men so that they hunger for him. Corpus Christi—the feast of the bread of life—is a good opportunity to reflect on the hunger which people suffer: hunger for truth, for justice, for unity, and for peace. To meet the hunger for peace we have to repeat what Saint Paul said: Christ is our peace, *pax nostra*.[19] The desire for truth should remind us that Jesus is the way, the truth, and the life.[20] Those who aspire to unity should be shown Christ, who prays that we will all be *consummati in unum*: "made perfectly one."[21] Hunger for justice should lead us to the original source of harmony among mankind: the fact that we are, and know ourselves to be, sons of the Father, brothers.

Peace, truth, unity, justice. How difficult it often seems to eliminate the barriers to human harmony! And yet we Christians are called to bring about that miracle of brotherhood. We must work so that everyone with God's grace can live in a

Christian way, "bearing one another's burdens,"[22] keeping the commandment of love which is the bond of perfection and the essence of the law.[23]

We cannot deny that a great deal remains to be done. On one occasion, when he was looking perhaps at the swaying wheatfields, Jesus said to his disciples: "The harvest is plentiful, but the laborers are few; pray therefore the Lord of the harvest to send out laborers into his harvest."[24] Now, as then, laborers are needed to bear "the burden of the day and the scorching heat."[25] And if we, the laborers, are not faithful, there will come to pass what was described by the prophet Joel: "The fields are laid waste, the ground mourns; because the grain is destroyed, the wine fails, the oil languishes. Be confounded, O tillers of the soil, wail, O winedressers, for the wheat and the barley, because the harvest of the field has perished."[26]

There is no harvest if we are not ready for constant, generous work, which can be long and tiring: ploughing the land, sowing the seed, weeding the fields, reaping and threshing.... The kingdom of God is fashioned in history, in time. Our Lord has entrusted this task to us, and no one can feel exempt. Today, as we adore Christ in the Eucharist, let us remember that the time has not yet come for resting. The day's work must go on.

It is written in the book of Proverbs: "He who tills his land will have plenty of bread."[27] Let us apply this passage to our spiritual life. If we do not work God's land, are not faithful to the divine mission of giving ourselves to others, helping them recognize Christ, we will find it very difficult to understand what the eucharistic bread is. No one values something which does not cost an effort. In order to value and love the holy Eucharist, we must follow Jesus' way. We must be grain; we must die to ourselves and rise full of life and give an abundant yield: a hundredfold![28]

Christ's way can be summed up in one word: love. If we are to love, we must have a big heart and share the concerns of those around us. We must be able to forgive and understand; we must sacrifice ourselves, with Jesus Christ, for all souls. If we love Christ's heart, we shall learn to serve others and we shall defend the truth clearly, lovingly. If we are to love in this way, we need to root out of our individual lives everything which is an obstacle to Christ's life in us: attachment to our own comfort, the temptation to selfishness, the tendency to be the center of everything. Only by reproducing in ourselves the word of Christ can we transmit it to others. Only by experiencing the death of the grain of wheat can we work in the heart of the world, transforming it from within, making it fruitful.

CHRISTIAN OPTIMISM

We may sometimes be tempted to think that this is very nice but an impossible dream. I have spoken to you about renewing your faith and your hope. Remain steadfast, with an absolute certainty that our longings will be satisfied through the wonders of God. However, it is essential that we anchor ourselves, truly, in the Christian virtue of hope. Let us not get used to the miracles which are happening before our eyes, especially the wonderful fact that our Lord comes down each day into the priest's hands. Jesus wants us to remain wide awake, so that we are convinced of his power and can hear once more his promise: "Follow me and I will make you become fishers of men";[29] you will be effective and attract souls to God. We should therefore trust our Lord's words: get into the boat, take the oars, hoist the sails and launch out into this sea of the world which Christ gives us as an inheritance. "Put out into the deep and let down your nets for a catch."[30] The apostolic zeal which Christ has put in our hearts must not be diminished or extinguished by a false humility. Maybe we experience the dead weight of our personal failings, but our Lord takes into account our mistakes. In his merciful gaze he realizes that we are creatures with limitations, weaknesses, and imperfections, that we are inclined to sin. But he tells us to fight, to acknowledge our weaknesses, not to be afraid, but to repent and foster a desire to improve.

We must also remember that we are only instruments. "What is Apollo? What is Paul? They are servants who brought the faith to you. Even the different ways in which they brought it were assigned to them by the Lord. I did the planting, Apollo the watering, but God gave the growth."[31] The teaching, the message which we have to communicate, has in its own right an infinite effectiveness which comes not from us, but from Christ. It is God himself who is bent on bringing about salvation, on redeeming the world.

We must, then, have faith and not be dispirited. We must not be stopped by any kind of human calculation. To overcome the obstacles we have to throw ourselves into the task so that the very effort we make will open up new paths. Personal holiness, giving oneself to God, is the one cure which overcomes any difficulty.

Being holy means living exactly as our Father in Heaven wants us to live. You will say that it is difficult. It is. The ideal is a very high one. And yet it is also easy. It is within our reach. When a person becomes ill, there may be no appropriate medicine. But in supernatural affairs, it is not like that. The medicine is always at hand. It is Jesus Christ, present in the holy Eucharist, and he also gives us his grace in the other sacraments which he established.

Let us say again, in word and in action: "Lord, I trust in you; your ordinary providence, your help each day, is all I need." We do not have to ask God to perform great miracles. Rather, we have to beg him to increase our faith, to enlighten our intellect and strengthen our will. Jesus always stays by our side and is always himself.

Ever since I began to preach, I have warned people against a certain mistaken sense of holiness. Don't be afraid to know your real self. That's right, you are made of clay. Don't be worried. For you and I are sons of God—and that is the right way of being made divine. We are chosen by a divine calling from all eternity: "The Father chose us in Christ before the foundation of the world, that we should be holy and blameless before him."[32] We belong especially to God, we are his instruments in spite of our great personal shortcomings. And we will be effective if we do not lose this awareness of our own weakness. Our temptations give us the measure of our own weakness.

If you feel depressed when you experience, perhaps in a very vivid way, your own pettiness, then is the time to abandon yourself completely and obediently into God's hands. There is a story about a beggar meeting Alexander the Great and asking him for alms. Alexander stopped and instructed that the man be given the government of five cities. The beggar, totally confused and taken aback, exclaimed: "I didn't ask for that much." And Alexander replied: "You asked like the man you are: I give like the man I am."

Even in moments when we see our limitations clearly, we can and should look at God the Father, God the Son, and God the Holy Spirit, and realize that we share in God's own life. There is never reason to look back.[33] The Lord is at our side. We have to be faithful and loyal; we have to face up to our obligations and we will find in Jesus the love and the stimulus we need to understand other people's faults and overcome our own. In this way even depression—yours, mine, anyone's—can also be a pillar for the kingdom of Christ.

Let us recognize our infirmity but confess the power of God. The Christian life has to be shot through with optimism, joy, and the strong conviction that our Lord wishes to make use of us. If we feel part of the Church, if we see ourselves sustained by the rock of Peter and by the action of the Holy Spirit, we will decide to fulfill the little duty of every moment. We will sow a little each day, and the granaries will overflow.

We must finish these minutes of prayer. Savoring in the intimacy of your soul the infinite goodness of God, realize that Christ is going to make himself really present in the Host, with his body, his blood, his soul, and his divinity. Adore him reverently, devoutly; renew in his presence the sincere offerings of your love. Don't be afraid to tell him that you love him. Thank him for giving you this daily proof of his tender mercy, and encourage yourself to go to Communion in a spirit of trust. I am awed by this mystery of Love. Here is the Lord seeking to use my heart as a throne, committed never to leave me, provided I don't run away.

Comforted by Christ's presence and nourished by his body, we will be faithful during our life on earth and then we will be victors with Jesus and his Mother in Heaven. "O death, where is your victory? O death, where is your sting? . . . Thanks be to God, who gives us the victory through our Lord Jesus Christ." [34]

NOTES

The Eucharist: Mystery of Faith and Love

1. Jn 13:1.
2. Lk 22:15.
3. Jn 6:69.
4. Jn 6:70.
5. See Jn 13:25.
6. Hymn *Pange, lingua.*
7. See hymn *Adoro te devote.*
8. See hymn *Ave, verum.*
9. See hymn *O sacrum convivium.*
10. Gen 1:26.
11. Jn 14:23.
12. *De fide orthodoxa*, 13 (PG 94, 1139).
13. Roman Missal, offertory, invocation to the Holy Spirit.
14. Ibid., prayer preparing for communion.
15. Ibid., offertory, offering to the Blessed Trinity.
16. Ibid., prayer before the final blessing.
17. Mal 1:11.
18. See Saint Thomas, S. Th., III, q. 65, a. 3.
19. *Catechesis*, 22, 3.
20. Jn 17:23.
21. *In Ioannis Evangelium tractatus*, 26, 13 (PL 35, 1613).
22. Saint Cyprian, *De dominica oratione*, 23 (PL 4, 553).
23. See Rev 5:9.
24. Hymn *Adoro te, devote:*
    praesta meae menti de te vivere,
    et te illi semper dulce sapere.
25. Mt 20:28.
26. Mt 7:21.
27. Mt 8:2: *Domine, si vis, potes me mundare.*

28. Jn 7:37.
29. Jn 15:15.
30. Jn 15:13.
31. See Jn 11:43; Lk 5:24.
32. Jn 13:15.

On the Feast of Corpus Christi

1. Mt 13:3–8.
2. 1 Cor 12:27: *Vos estis corpus Christi et membra de membro.*
3. Jn 13:1.
4. 1 Cor 11:23–25.
5. Sequence *Lauda Sion*.
6. Ibid.
7. Ibid.
8. Ibid.
9. Saint Augustine, *In Ioannis Evangelium tractatus*, 26, 20 (PL 35, 1616).
10. Hymn *Sacris solemnis*.
11. Jn 15:5.
12. Acts 2:42.
13. *In Matthaeum homiliae*, 82, 1 (PG 58, 700).
14. Rom 12:2: *in novitate sensus*.
15. 2 Cor 2:15: *bonus odor Christi*.
16. Jn 12:32.
17. See Jn 12:24.
18. 1 Cor 10:17.
19. Eph 2:14.
20. See Jn 14:6.
21. Jn 17:23.
22. Gal 6:2.
23. See Col 3:14; Rom 13:10.
24. Mt 9:38.
25. Mt 20:12.
26. Joel 1:10–11.
27. Prov 12:11.
28. See Mk 4:8.
29. Mk 1:17.
30. Lk 5:4: *Duc in altum et laxate retia vestra in capturam.*

31. 1 Cor 3:4–6.
32. Eph 1:4.
33. See Lk 9:62.
34. 1 Cor 15:55, 57.